ORIENTAL RUGS

Text by
D.M. Field

Crescent Books

New York

Endpapers and title page: **Detail of a Tabriz carpet, 19th century (Milan, private collection) and a modern Kayseri carpet with a pattern of cypresses.**

Designed and produced by Editions Minerva SA

First English edition published by Editions Minerva SA

Copyright © 1983 by Minerva Editions S.A., Geneve.

This 1983 edition is published by Crescent Books. Distributed by Crown Publishers, Inc.

Printed in Italy

Library of Congress Cataloging in Publication Data

ISBN: 0-517-424827

INTRODUCTION

The appeal of oriental carpets, or rugs as they are called in the United States, is extraordinarily wide. It is not necessary to be an expert in this arcane art form in order to appreciate their very obvious virtues, both aesthetic and practical. And, fortunately, they are one of the very few hand-crafted objects which are not yet too expensive for people of average financial resources to own. Naturally, you cannot go into a dealer's shop and buy a 17th-century Persian garden carpet —not even if your name is Rothschild —but you can buy a very fine rug, made by methods which have changed very little in 500 years, which will not only give you a great deal of pleasure as it lies on your floor but will also (unless you have been unlucky or foolish) retain or increase its real value as time goes by.

The popularity of oriental carpets in the West, which dates from the Renaissance, has never been greater than it is today. It is, therefore, something of a paradox that our knowledge of this wonderful craft is, in fact, very patchy. About a century ago, Sir C. Purdon Clarke, who was in his time director or assistant director of both the Victoria and Albert Museum in London and the Metropolitan Museum in New York (two of the finest public collections of oriental carpets in the West), remarked that 'there is probably no industry about which we know less bibliographically, and the paucity of reference is more extraordinary as it is not confined to the works of remote ages but is continued to our own time.' Even more extraordinary, this statement is still broadly true. Except for the work of one or two German scholars, there have been no really important advances in our knowledge of oriental carpets in this century.

At the deepest level, the subject of oriental carpets is extremely complex. There are, of course, experts and rich connoisseurs who can tell you exactly in what village, or by which tribe (even family), a particular rug was made. They can explain with more or less confidence the true significance of the colours, patterns and motifs. Nevertheless, the whole subject is in scholarly terms ill-defined and open to argument. Practically every statement made by one expert will be contradicted by another. This extends to matters which you might expect to be fundamental. For example, here are two statements from two books on oriental carpets, by acknowledged experts, written in the past twelve years, concerning the town of Senneh, or Sehna, which gave its name to one of the two types of knot used in oriental carpets.

'In spite of the common use of the term Senneh knot to indicate the Persian knot, it is, in fact, the Turkish knot which is used in Senneh carpets.'

And here is our second expert: '[Sehna] has given its name to the Sehna or Persian knot which is used [there].'

Apart from the generally dodgy nature of the subject, this disagreement illustrates the fact that in very fine, dense carpets (as Senneh carpets are) it is much harder to distinguish which knot was used than you might expect after reading the instructions of the experts to push back the pile and examine an individual knot. On finely made carpets this is practically impossible !

There is no need, here, to venture into the more abstruse —indeed mystical — aspects of carpet-making. But it is important to remember that virtually any general statement about oriental carpets can be qualified if not contradicted. Thus, it is broadly true that floral carpets come from Persia (Iran) and geometrical ones from Turkey, the Caucasus or other adjoining areas, but it is also true that some floral carpets were made in Turkey and that geometrical patterns predominate in some parts of Persia.

Left : Caucasian carpet, Kuba, 18th century. The large X pattern is characteristic of a type of antique Kuba rug, and distinguishes them from other Caucasian carpets, in which patterns generally are widely shared. *Above:* Caucasian carpet, southern Caucasus; Villa Medicea di Fiorale, Florence.

HISTORY

For essential purposes the history of oriental carpets goes back about 500 years. Nevertheless, they were made at a much earlier date than that, and any account of their history, however brief, must begin with the famous Pazyryk carpet, discovered by Russian archaeologists in 1949 in a high valley of the Altai Mountains near the Mongolian border. Water leading into the burial chamber had formed a thick layer of ice in which the carpet had been preserved for 2,500 years.

The Pazyryk carpet, probably made by Scythian nomads and now in the Hermitage Museum, Leningrad, is approximately two metres square, hand-knotted with the Turkish knot and superbly worked, with splendid figures of horsemen and elks in the border bands. The colours naturally are so badly faded that their original appearance is hard to judge. Nevertheless, the Pazyryk carpet, which is nearly 2,000 years older than the next survival of comparable quality, demonstrates that the art was already well established 500 years before the birth of Christ.

Woven carpets are probably nearly as old as the loom, which was in use in ancient Egypt by about 3000 BC. The Egyptians certainly used textiles —woven but probably not knotted— to spread on the floor, though whether they, the Chinese, or any of various other claimants 'invented' the carpet is a matter of argument. Since carpets are made of perishable materials, there is little surviving evidence, apart from the Pazyryk carpet and a number of other lucky freaks, until the Renaissance period.

There is, however, some evidence from sculptured reliefs and murals, which tend to show how ancient are the design of Near Eastern weavers. John Kimberley Mumford, in his *Oriental Rugs* (1902), claimed to have found in a New York dealer's stock in 1899 a Persian silk rug which closely reproduced an Assyrian design known from wall reliefs at Nineveh. 'The Armenian dealer laughed at it as uncouth, and said he had no idea of its meaning, Yet it linked the immediate present with the life of oldest Assyria, across the abyss of more than thirty centuries.'

There is no lack of indirect evidence from documentary sources. Numerous references to sumptuous carpets occur in the Bible and in the pages of Greek and Roman authors from Homer onwards. We are all familiar with Cleopatra's use of a carpet to invade the privacy of Julius Caesar.

It can safely be said that among the nomadic tribes of western Asia carpet-making was well established over 2,000 years ago. Carpets were the only form of furniture these people had, but they possessed an importance far greater than their practical function. Each knot, it was said, represented a thought, and the pattern was an expression of its makers' beliefs and traditions.

Persia (Iran) is rightly considered the heartland of the oriental carpet, so much so that at one time all such carpets were loosely described as 'Persian'. It appears that carpet-making was already an established, conscious art in the time of Cyrus the Great, whose tomb, when he died in 529 BC, was covered with precious carpets. Carpet production is mentioned in Persia under the Sassanid dynasty (AD 226-641), and the famous garden carpet known as the 'Springtime of Chosroes' (surviving only in admiring descriptions) dates from the later Sassanid period. During succeeding centuries there is little evidence of the craft, though there can be no doubt it continued at least at a fairly humble level.

The Mongol conquest in the 13th century was indirectly responsible for introducing some Chinese motifs into Persian carpets. Carpet patterns are less autonomous than is sometimes assumed, and there was considerable interchange at various times. Since the 18th century Western motifs, often transformed beyond easy identification, have figured prominently.

Above left: **Detail of a 16th-century Persian hunting carpet, which shows the combination of highly naturalistic animals with more stylized motifs.** *Above:* **Detail from Holbein's painting,** *The Ambassadors,* **in the National Gallery, London. The Turkish carpet is depicted with the same devoted attention to detail as the navigational instruments.**

After some seven centuries of alien rule, the native Safavid dynasty was established at the end of the 15th century and within a few years Persian carpet-making entered its most glorious period (also the earliest period from which carpets actually survive in some numbers).

Culminating under the greatest of the Safavids, Shah Abbas (1586-1628), Persia underwent a 'renaissance' of all the arts, including carpet-making ; carpet design, at least at the court workshops in Isfahan, was closely related to painting.

Carpet experts show an uncommon measure of agreement in assigning the first among carpets to the famous piece known as the Ardebil carpet, which is now in the Victoria and Albert Museum, London. Unusually, though not uniquely, the Ardebil carpet bears an inscription giving the name of the maker or — possibly— the man who gave it to the Ardebil Mosque, as well as the date of manufacture — 1540 in the Christian calendar. The Ardebil carpet, approximately 12×6 metres, has a silk warp and weft and a wool pile with about 350 knots to the square inch, the Persian knot being employed. Two other magnificent carpets from this famous mosque —where Shah Ismail, founder of the Safavid dynasty, is buried — are in the Metropolitan Museum, New York. Another famous carpet of the same period, also signed, is the hunting carpet (bearing figures of huntsmen and animals on the field) in the Poldi Pezzoli Museum, Milan, which measures approximately 6×4 metres and was made un 1543.

Oriental carpets —particularly Turkish— were not unknown in medieval Europe. Indeed, some were made there, by the Moors in Spain who brought with them their Eastern looms and patterns. Their popularity during the renaissance, when they were more often used to cover tables than floors, is evident from the works of many painters. Indeed, Holbein has given his name to a type of carpet which appears frequently in his paintings. The 'Holbein' carpets probably came from Ushak, though they bear no relation to more recent carpets from that area.

Shah Abbas sent some young men to study art in Rome, which resulted in examples of Western influence in the design of Persian carpets. Soon afterwards, factories for making 'Turkish' carpets were set up at Arras and elsewhere in France.

It is important to remember that the Persian empire formerly occupied a much

The 'Ardebil' carpet, Persian, 1540; Victorian and Albert Museum, London. Probably the most famous carpet in the world, it was made in Kashan or Isfahan. The inscription (top) reads: 'I have no refuge in the world other than thy threshold. There is no place of protection for my head other than this door. The work of the slave of the threshold Maqsud the slave of the Holy Place of Kashan in the year 946.'

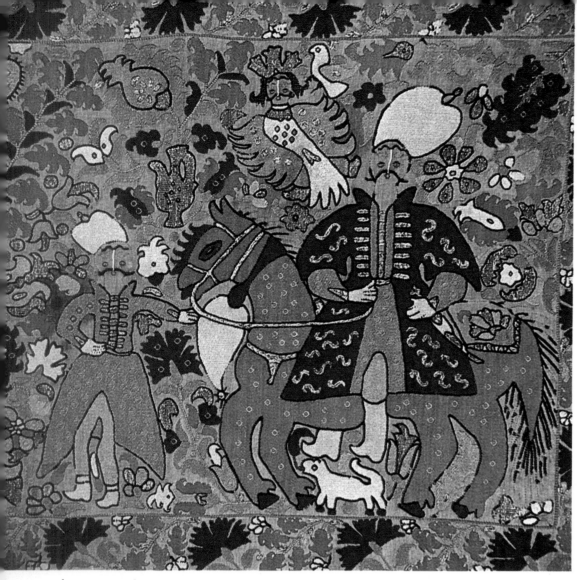

making in Persia became again the activity of village craftsmen and nomads; it did not regain its importance until the end of the century and, arguably, never achieved the distinction of the 16th century.

Production gradually increased, largely in response to Western demand, throughout the 19th century, and European and American entrepreneurs moved into the country to organize production for Western markets. By the end of the century, the one major change in the way oriental carpets have been made over the centuries was beginning to take effect. This was the introduction of chemical dyes, which were far cheaper than the traditional vegetable dyes in use hitherto —though, as we shall see, much less satisfactory.

The comparative ignorance of oriental carpets in the West as recently as a century ago is illustrated by the famous 'Polonaise' carpets, which were once believed to have been made in Poland by Persian craftsmen. They first came to public notice in 1878 when a group of them were exhibited at the Trocadero in Paris by a Polish nobleman, Prince Czartoryski. Of superb workmanship, with silk pile woven with gold and silver threads, they were, admittedly, unlike any other group of Persian carpets of their period (16th and 17th centuries). Quite a large number of these carpets can still be seen in various European museums, and it is now generally accepted that they originated as gifts to European rulers from the Safavid court. They were probably made at Kashan or at the royal workshops of Isfahan.

Throughout the series of conquests and upheavals that mark the history of western Asia, the carpet has always survived at some level. Interchange —peaceful or violent— brought new influences, though the constants remain in the infinitely various patterns. Striking artistic developments sometimes occurred in one area while another was showing signs of stagnation. Eventually, commercial pressures had more powerful effects than any social upheaval could cause. But even now, in spite of the stories about rugs bought in remote Eastern villages which on closer inspection bear the stamped imprint 'Made in Birmingham', there are still rugs and carpets being made in virtually the same way and with the same materials as they were centuries ago.

larger area than modern Iran. It included carpet-making centres which are now in Afghanistan, Pakistan and the Soviet Union: contemporary political frontiers are not of great significance to a craft that has been going on for thousands of years.

The beautiful Safavid capital of Isfahan was virtually destroyed during the Afghan invasions early in the 18th century, and the dynasty, which had become steadily less distinguished since the death of Shah Abbas, came to an end. Carpet-

Above left: **A quaint piece probably woven in the Balkans under Turkish rule; Benaki Museum, Athens. Left: However 'abstract' the pattern of antique oriental carpets, the motifs were not celebral geometric fantasies, but derived from sources in nature; Victoria and Albert Museum, London.**

TECHNIQUE

With certain exceptions, oriental carpets have a pile which is made by tying small knots of yarn on the warp threads. In general the warp and weft are cotton or (less often) wool or other material, and the pile is wool. Some of the finest examples are made of silk, but these are usually 'display' carpets, often given as a present from one ruler to another. Silk is less hard-wearing than wool, apart from being more costly.

In recent times carpets have been made in all shapes and sizes to suit Western markets. In their countries of origin they were used for many purposes —saddlebags, cushions, etc.— as well as floor coverings. But there are certain traditional shapes which derive partly from the size of the looms used and partly from the manner of arranging carpets on the floor.

The best-known is the prayer rug (making up probably the majority of

Above: **A nomadic Iranian weaver knotting a carpet on a horizontal loom. The implements in the foreground are used for beating down the weft threads.** *Right:* **A carpet taking shape at a carpet-making school in Isfahan. The bench is raised as work progresses.**

shears or scissors for clipping the pile.

In the last century a dealer from Smyrna (Izmir) tried to get the firm's craftsmen at Ushak, Ghiordes and other places to use a small steel rod fastened across the face of the warp, around which the knots were tied. A groove along the length of the rod received the knife blade as it cut the yarn. The circumference of the rod corresponded to the desired length of pile, and its effect was to reduce wastage in the final trimming from about 25 per cent to about 2 per cent. However, it slowed down the work, and since the reduction in waste was of no benefit to the weavers, only to their employers, they rejected the device.

Raw Materials. Sheep's wool is the commonest material for the pile and, among nomadic people (who don't stay put long enough to grow cotton) for the warp and weft as well. Camel hair and occasionally goat hair are also used.

The best wool comes from the shoulder and flank of the living sheep (wool from a dead animal is dull and stiff), and the fleece should have been combed in the winter and shorn in the spring. Traditionally, some of the finest wool comes from Kurdistan (western Persia and beyond). The wool must be carefully scoured and washed many times before spinning into yarn.

Knots. The prime characteristic of oriental carpets is that they are hand-knotted (small fingers are an advantage and children were once excessively employed). Two knots are employed: the Persian or Senneh knot and the Turkish or Ghiordes knot. They are sometimes called 'single' and double' knots, but this is misleading. In the Turkish knot, the yarn is looped over each of two warp threads, the ends emerging between them. In the Persian knot, the yarn is looped around one warp thread and under the adjacent one. The Turkish knot is slightly more secure and has, over the years, tended to displace the Persian knot. However, the Persian knot predominates in a large part of Persia itself and is also found east of the Caspian Sea.

Some modern carpets use *jufti* or false knots, which are exactly the same, Persian or Turkish, except that they treat two warp threads as one. The craftsman thus spans four threads with each knot instead of two, and the carpet, containing half as many knots, is finished in half the time; the effects on durability and appearance can easily be imagined.

Broadly speaking, the denser the pile

Turkish carpets) with its characteristic *mihrab* or prayer-niche pattern, the purpose of which is obvious. Other names, such as kelley (kellegi) and kenareh refer to a traditional Persian floor arrangement, in which three carpets, the central one (kelley) broader, were laid parallel, with a fourth laid at right angles at one end.

Looms. Carpets are made entirely by hand on a loom, of which traditionally there are two basic types, horizontal and vertical. The horizontal or ground loom of nomadic peoples consists of two wooden beams, with the warp threads stretched between them. When in use, the loom is braced by posts driven into the ground to which the beams are tied. When the tribe moves on, the whole thing can be rolled up into a bundle.

The simplest kind of vertical loom, still to be seen in many villages, is fixed upright against a wall, usually outside.

The warp threads are stretched vertically between two beams and the craftsman sits on a board, making lines of knots from the bottom. The board can be raised as he (or she) proceeds, keeping the work at a comfortable level.

This type of loom restricts the potential length of the carpet, and has long been superceded by a loom in which the warp threads run around the lower beam and return to the upper beam, doubling the length. Nowadays, the loom usually has roller beams, which allow the completed part of the carpet to be rolled up on the lower beam while the warp unwinds from the upper beam. Length is thus unrestricted.

Other tools. Apart from the loom, the craftsman's tools are few: a knife for cutting the yarn after each knot; a comb, nowadays commonly made of strips of metal, for beating down the weft threads after each row of knots, and a pair of

Washing the finished carpets. *Above:* In an Iranian village. The quality of the water is said to be important in assuring quality. *Below:* In the carpet-making centre of Nahadjan. Washing removes stiffness and restores the purity of the colours.

the better. The finest silk carpets are said to have the fantastic number of 2,000 knots to the square inch. The finest Persian wool carpets may have nearly half that number, but a carpet of average quality will have perhaps 150 to 180. This is still a very geat number: a craftsman tying about fifteen knots per minute in an average-quality carpet measuring 2×3 metres will hardly finish it in six months.

After each row of knots, one or two weft threads are woven on to the warp. After several rows of knots have been made, the pile is cropped, but not too close. The final cropping, which demands a high degree of skill, is done when the carpet is finished.

Finally, the carpet, completed with selvedge (to secure the edges) and fringe (the ends of the warp threads, traditionally left very long in nomadic rugs), is

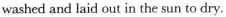

washed and laid out in the sun to dry.

The old nomadic and village rugs were made with nothing to go on except a general idea —itself the product of long tradition— in the mind of the maker. Examined closely, they invariably reveal slight inconsistencies. More complicated designs — in the time of Abbas the Great often the work of court artists — are prepared on a cartoon, hung from the loom. Sometimes one person will call out the knots to fellow-workers.

Above left: **After washing, the carpets are laid out to dry in the sun, a crucial test of colour fastness.** *Above:* **A corner of the carpet bazaar at Qum.** *Left:* **Child labour is now illegal in Iran, but in earlier times the weaving was often done by young children, whose small fingers perhaps permitted finer knotting.**

Killims. Like the Caucasian rugs known as Sumaks (briefly described in a later chapter) killims are distinguished from other oriental carpets in having no knotted pile. They are built up in the same way as a tapestry, the pattern being made from coloured weft threads and, although there is normally a 'right' and a 'wrong' side to a killim, the pattern is visible on both sides. Although good killims are very tough, they are clearly less suitable than knotted-pile carpets for floor coverings. In the East they had a variety of uses, notably as a protective wrapper for a bundle of more fragile possessions, though they are also spread on the floor.

The earliest-known killim was discovered in 1960 near the ancient site of Troy and dated to 2500 BC (2,000 years earlier than the Pazyryk carpet). Although it disintegrated on being exposed to the air, the design and even the colours could be reconstructed. It was not significantly different from killims woven today!

Since killims are less obviously glamorous than knotted-pile carpets, they have been largely ignored until recent years. This has had the great advantage that killims have seldom been woven for the export market and are therefore more 'authentic'.

Kilim rug. This method of weaving is also known as the slit-tapestry technique. The word *kilim* is apparently related to an Arabic word meaning 'curtain', and the earliest use of these rugs was no doubt as decorative hangings. They can also be seen (for instance) wrapped around the household goods on the back of a horse or camel.

COLOURS AND PATTERNS

Apart from the method of manufacture, the most distinctive and appealing characteristics of oriental carpets are their colours and patterns. The wandering Turkoman shepherds over 2,000 years ago no doubt used wool in its natural shades, which are quite various, ranging from white to black with many intermediate shades of brown. At some remote time they took to colouring the wool artificially and evolved an extraordinarily rich range of colours from natural products. These traditional colours, employed universally until the late 19th century, are known as vegetable dyes, since the great majority (though not in fact all) are derived from plants.

Dyeing. The art of dyeing is a true 'mystery' in the medieval sense of the word, an esoteric craft requiring years of experience and a knowledge of processes not easily learned. 'It is not unusual', wrote one Victorian authority, 'for a master dyer to be skilled in some hundreds of shades of red, any one of which he can set about compounding at a moment's notice, without thought or reference to any "aids" or "authorities".

In Eastern villages, where the weaving was done by women, the dyeing was invariably done by men, and in dyers' families the secret was handed down through the generations, from father to son. Some villages cultivated plants for dyeing exclusively and carefully guarded the process from outsiders. Dyers held a revered status in society, like that of blacksmiths in the tribal villages of Africa.

However, and in spite of the enthusiastic appraisal quoted above, it is virtually impossible to reproduce precisely the same colour in separate dyeings by the traditional methods. There are too many variables, like the quality of the water used, the strength of the sunlight in which the skeins of dyed wool are hung to dry, as well as the dye itself. As a result an old carpet (made before about 1900) will nearly always show slight variations in any large area of plain colour. There is a technical name for these faint streaks, *abrash*. Although strictly speaking it is of course an imperfection, it is actually valued as a manifestation of human art, as distinct from mechanical craft, like brush marks on an oil painting or marks of the sculptor's chisel in a marble statue.

When the modern synthetic dyes are used, this effect does not appear. Unfortunately, it can be simulated; but the trick

Two prayer rugs. The Persian piece (*above*) is a comparatively modern rug (early 20th century) from Tabriz. *Below*: Caucasian prayer rug. The design of prayer rugs, which have the form of an arch or mihrab, is dictated by religious convention.

can often be detected by examining the pile which, in synthetically dyed carpets, may reveal a tell-tale change of colour at the surface. It is, for instance, not uncommon to find that yellow on the surface is green in the deep pile —the effects of light having removed the blue component of the original green.

Vegetable Dyes. The commonest colour in oriental carpets, more particularly Turkish, is red. The main source of red in recent times has been cochineal, an insect which was cultivated in Central America in pre-Columbian times. Before its introduction to the East, Persian dyers used another insect called the kermes, which belongs to the same family. The stationary habits and curious appearance of the female (the source of the dye) led to its being long mistaken, in Europe anyway, for a type of parasitic plant growth.

Red was also obtained from the roots of madder, a family which includes the coffee plant. By boiling and pounding, a colour sometimes called Turkey Red was obtained, more brilliant than the deep crimson of kermes or the carmine shade of cochineal. By combining these with various other ingredients, different shades and colours could be produced.

The main source of blue was indigo. The famous Persian Blue, which proved so difficult to imitate, came from dyeing with indigo over madder. Yellow was derived from a variety of herbs, roots and berries. A brilliant yellow known as weld (or woald) came from the plant of the same name.

Besides thoses primary colours, there were many other dyes produced from various plants and logwood, as well as by mixing the primary colours. Green, rather rare in Turkish carpets but more common in Persian, could be obtained by mixing yellow and blue derived from copper sulphate; brown by mixing madder and yellow, or from walnuts. Brown also occurred in natural form, as did black. When wool was dyed black (relatively uncommon, as black was not much used), a slightly acid dye was used which damaged the wool. In some old carpets, black areas are noticeably more worn, and the same result is sometimes evident in green areas where copper sulphate was used. Otherwise, vegetable dyes had no harmful effects on the wool.

Synthetic Dyes. The discovery of aniline, an oily liquid derived from coal (and, incidentally, a deadly poison) in Europe in 1856 marked the beginning of

the synthetic-dye industry. The first aniline dye marketed was a magnificent purple, and it was soon followed by others (not all of which, though generically described as aniline dyes, actually contained aniline). The aniline dyes, very cheap and easily obtainable, reached the Near East before the end of the 19th century. Despite local efforts to exclude them —a Persian dyer found using aniline dyes was liable to have his hand cut off—

The outstanding characteristics of oriental carpets are, of course, pattern and colour. The latter quality is hard to convey in photographs, despite modern photographic and printing skills, and this is especially true of antique Persian carpets, such as the magnificent animal carpet at *right,* in which colour tones are extraordinarily subtle. Colours do also fade, but in antique carpets of high quality they seem never to lose their integrity and, in well-preserved specimens, may even benefit from the gentle ageing process.

by the First World War they had largely replaced vegetable dyes. The latter are still used occasionally today, though less often than the assurances of dealers would lead the customer to suppose.

Once an indigenous craft acquires large export potential, it degenerates. Recent history has often demonstrated this inescapable fact. By the end of the 19th century, oriental carpets were suffering in quality from the massive demands of the Western market, and already traditional centres, famous for their exquisite work of the past, were turning out cheap and faithless reproductions of their ancestors' masterpieces. Nevertheless, fine carpets comparable with their predecessors were still being produced in fair numbers. However, the advent of synthetic dyes was little short of disastrous.

The disadvantages of the early aniline dyes —shared, though to a lesser extent, by more recent dyes which do not contain aniline— are several. In the first place, they are less stable. All colours fade in light, but vegetable dyes gradually acquire a more mellow appearance which explains the harmonious effect of antique carpets (using the word antique to mean a carpet made by the traditional methods, not —as dealers tend to use it— for any carpet that is not brand-new). Aniline dyes fade much faster and may indeed change colour completely — green turning to yellow, as described above— producing an effect quite different from that intended by the weaver. Worse still, aniline dyes have a deleterious effect on the wool itself. They dry out the pile, which may quite rapidly lose that mysterious lustre which is so admirable a characteristic of good carpets. The fibres become brittle and more susceptible to wear. Whereas an antique carpet, reasonably well cared for, will last for generations with no significant loss in quality, an aniline-dyed carpet may show signs of wear after only a few years.

The Significance of Colour. Colours, like patterns, were not chosen by the weaver merely because they looked pretty but because of their symbolic associations. Green for example, the colour of Muḥammad's banner, is a sacred colour in Islam; it is therefore seldom found in carpets (where it would be trodden on) made by the stricter Muslim peoples, though in Shi'ite Persia it is not so unusual. Black, the colour of evil and sorrow, is naturally uncommon. Red, on the other hand, is the great life-giving colour, and is accordingly popular. White may (though not always) signify mourning; the deep blue of pure indigo is the

The borders of all Oriental carpets reveal as much artistic refinement as their central medaillons.

colour of solitude, while the characteristic Mughal Blue of some old Indian carpets is an imperial colour, like the purple made by the ancient Phoenicians from seashells (a lost art) or the gold of China.

Patterns. Those who have made a serious study of oriental carpets can understand the different traditions and beliefs of the people who made them. The main carpet-making regions each have their own heritage to which they remained constant for many centuries. This is still largely true, in spite of the great changes of recent times — greater mobility and interchange (including the forced uprooting and scarttering of carpet-marking communities), commercialization of the craft, and the need to adjust to the taste of Western markets. Today, however, it is necessary to keep an eye open for reproductions of a famous type made in some industrial centre far removed, both

Left and above : Examples of border patterns: Pergame (18 th cent.), Armenia (19th cent.), Anatolia (19th cent.), Saruk (19th cent.), Caucasus (19th cent.), Ushak (17th cent.), Oriental Persia (end of the 19th cent.).

geographically and spiritually, from its place of origine.

Some patterns are characteristic of not only a particular region or district but even of an individual family. In theory (though rarely in practice), it is possible with an antique carpet to trace its origin very precisely, possibly to an individual weaver. It is true that foreign influences are by no means confined to the recent period or to the effects of Western demand, but occur throughout history. The appearance of Chinese motifs following the Mongol conquest has already been mentioned, and French designs made a considerable impact in the 18th century, especially after the oriental craftsmen employed at the Savonnerie works in France had returned to their native land, bringing French patterns with them. Nevertheless, these alien influences never altered the basic character of the carpets in which they appeared.

Broadly, oriental carpet design can be divided into two types —geometric and floral. The floral carpets are, pre-eminently, the product of the workshops of Persia and India. In design they are closely related to contemporary developments in Islamic art, particularly miniature painting.

Geometric designs are, indeed, fre-

quently derived from natural phenomena, including flowers. But this origin is often not evident to the inexperienced observer. The patterns are made up of straight lines —vertical, horizontal, diagonal— and the overall design tends to be relatively simple, with motifs repeated in series. Caucasian carpets are —with few exceptions— geometric in design, as are most Turkish carpets. Except in relatively modern carpets designed for export, representations of living creatures, human or animal, are not normally found in Turkish carpets. This is the result of a strict interpretation of the Koran which (like the Bible) condemns false images. In certain Muslim societies, this prohibition was very strictly intepreted, to exclude all representations of human beings or animals.

In recent times general opinion tended to regard floral carpets as the finest expression of the art, and geometric rugs, associated particularly with simple nomads, were regarded as 'primitive'. A contrary school of opinion held that the great floral carpets of the Safavid era actually represented a step towards decadence. Neither view cuts much ice today. However, there is a widespread tendency in modern society to prefer 'folk' art to the art of courts and princes.

MOTIFS

Il would be a thankless task to attempt to list all the charesteristic motifs and designs of oriental carpets. Not only are there an enormous number, their forms are capable of countless variations. Moreover, there is widespread disagreement even among scholars regarding their origin and significance, and indeed their names. One Victorian authority held that all the patterns found in oriental carpets are derived from the lotus. Would that it were so simple !

All design is founded ultimately on nature, and many of even the starkest geometrical motifs are stylized representations of living forms, immediately recognizeable to the carpet-makers though much less obvious to us. A certain motif may look like, say, the ground plan for a civic centre, but it actually represents perhaps a dragon or a bird. All representations of plants animals have a symbolic meaning, though their precise significance cannot always be casilè judged ; moreover, things have different meanings in different places. Certain objects, however, have a special universal meaning. The common motif of the tree of life is a religious symbol conveying the power of god and the continuance of life after death.

Some motifs, though of controversial origin, are found very widely. Perhaps the best-known is the *boteh* motif, like a pear with its top twisted to one side, which was adopted in the West as the familiar Paisley pattern. It is variously referred to as pear, almond, fir cone, flame, and a dozen other names which reflect uncertainty of its origin. It resembles, as much as anything, young leaves of the popular house plant, *hoya carnosa*, which is a native of Persia. It occurs in many different forms, and is especially notable in Mir rugs of central-western Persia, where it occupies the whole field in rows (and is hence sometimes called the *boteh mir*). On some floral carpets it appears as a spray of flowers, with no obvious outline, while in Caucasian rugs it adopts a rigidly geometric form.

The *gul* ('rose' in Persian) is the basis of the slightly rounded octagonal forms found most frequently in Bukhara carpets but also in many other regions. The *herati* design, named for the city of Herat, is perhaps the commonest in oriental carpets generally : it consists of a central rosette in a diamond along the sides of which are vaguely fish-like forms which are responsible for the alternative name, fish pattern, though in fact they are leaves, not fish. The *Shah Abbassi* design has a central flower (?pineapple) enclosed in a wreath, frequently on a deep red background. The *mina khami*, characteristic of western Persia, consists of a series of flowers linked by vines in a lattice-like pattern.

A great variety of other motifs, called crosses, diamonds, eggs, baskets, wineglasses and many other more or less doubtful names are also found. Variations of the Greek key or Chinese fret, including swastikas and the latch-hook or running-dog motif, appear in the borders of carpets. Many of them are difficult to describe in words, while drawings of them tend to mislead since there are so many variations on each theme.

Two 19th-century Persian carpets, examples of the wealth of decorative motifs evolved from basically simple forms. Unlike Western art, Muslim art avoids limits and outlines: patterns suggest infinity.

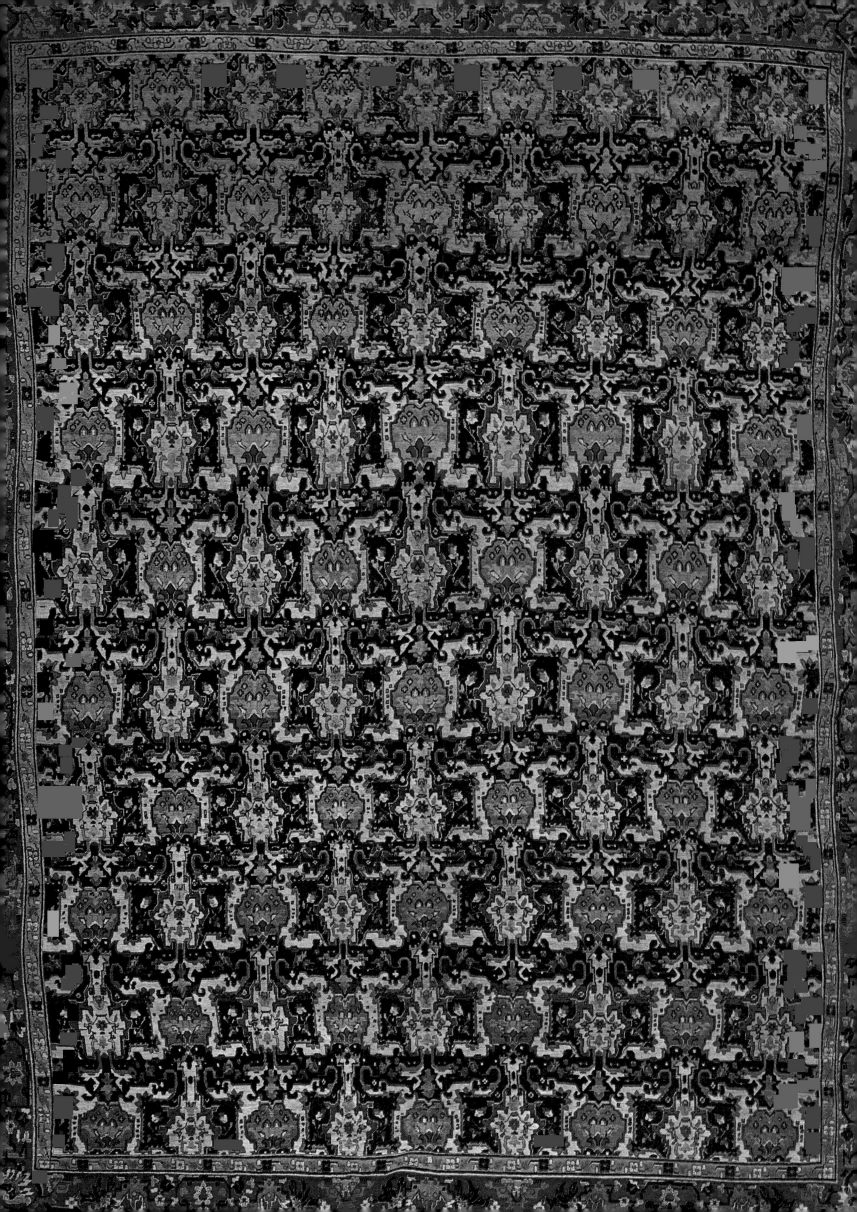

PERSIA

Persia, or Iran, is the outstanding country among the producers of oriental carpets. In the past it was the source of the finest examples ever seen, and it has continued to be the chief producer, both in quantity and quality, in modern times. Until the recent upheavals in that country, about 75 per cent of the world market in oriental rugs and carpets was supplied by Persian weavers.

According to one school of thought, the Persians adopted the art of carpet-making from the neighbouring tribes of Turkestan and Asia Minor, and transformed it in accordance with developments in Persian art generally. The splendour of the colours and the naturalistic decoration were inspired by miniatures and by the fine art of book-binding. The main feature of the design introduced by the Persian carpet-makers was the central medallion, infinitely various, with the design often repeated in the corners. The garden carpet and the allied hunting carpet represented the peak of Persian art in the Safavid era. A few masterpieces, like the Ardebil carpet in London and the hunting carpet in Milan, bear the names of their originators, though this is uncommon. Others include lines of poetry or verses from the Koran.

There are literally hundreds of names attached to the varieties of Persian carpets. Some of them are repetitive, representing nothing more than disagreements about spelling; some of them are of villages within the same area producing virtually identical carpets. But even without these, there are about seventy generally recognized types. Further complications arise from the fact that in some places the type of carpet made has changed completely (usually for the worse) at some point in time, and, even more confusingly, from the production of a named type of carpet at a commercial centre far removed from the original and bearing no relation to it except, perhaps, in general pattern. In the past the name of a place has sometimes become attached to a certain type of carpet erroneously —perhaps because the place concerned acted as a distribution centre for the manufactures of villages that were sometimes far distant— while dealers sometimes employ place names an an indication of quality rather than origin. Considerable disagreement often arises concerning exactly what kind of carpets were made in a particular centre. Finally, although all or nearly all traditional carpet-making centres seem to have continued in operation until the present, it must be remembered that the quality of current production is seldom the same as in antique examples.

For these reasons, the classification of Persian carpets is a far from exact business. But, bearing these qualifications in mind, the main types of Persian carpet can be briefly summarized as follows.

Ardebil. This is the town in northwest Persia which is associated with several famous 16th-century carpets made in the reign of Shah Tahmasp or Shah Abbas. Those carpets, however, were not made in Ardebil but (probably) in Kashan. Modern Ardebil carpets have no connection with them, being Caucasian in type, with geometric patterns, sometimes on an ivory ground and with elaborate borders made up of many bands. The pile tends to be coarse and the knot density (Turkish knot) correspondingly low.

Right: **Detail of the Ardebil carpet (see page 5), showing the central medallion with pendant 'lozenges'. It was not, of course, made in Ardebil and has no connection with modern Ardebil carpets.** *Below:* **a modern Persian kilim.**

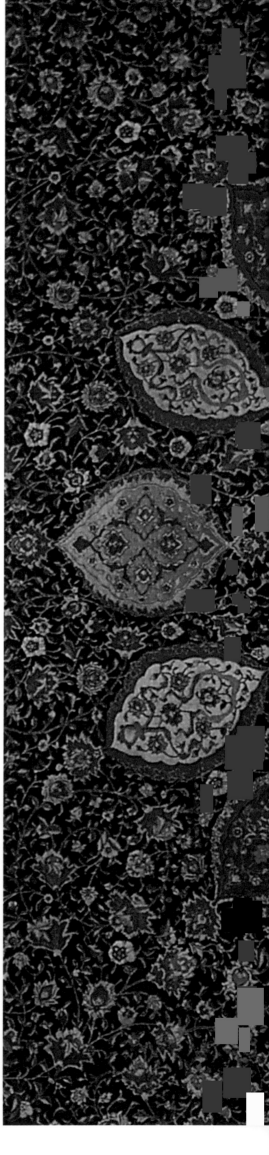

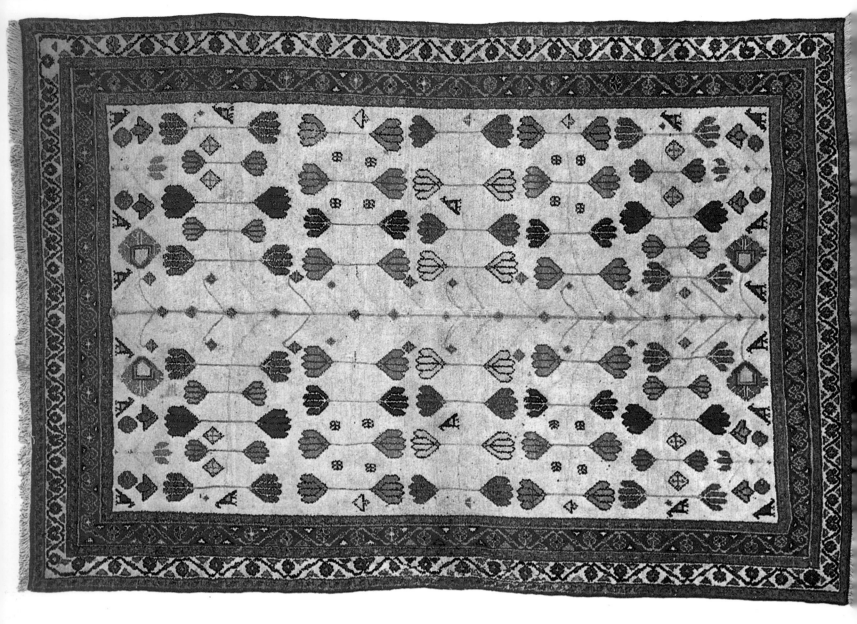

Bakhtiari. A region north of the Persian Gulf where modern carpets are made by people of nomadic origin originally from the Hamadan area. They also show the influence of nearby Isfahan. The latter type, which use the Persian rather than the Turkish knot characteristic of other Bakhtiari designs, are floral with a central medallion, though more formal in appearance than Isfahan carpets. Otherwise, the most typical Bakhtiari patterns are a field divided into a series of more or less geometric figures, each one slightly different, and a repeated all-over design of formalized flowers or the boteh motif.

Bijar. The town of Bijar in northwest Persia has had a sorry history in the 20th century; many people died during a famine after the First World War. Modern Bijar carpets are not very common, and though they follow the old traditions are often rather glaring in colour. Antique Bijar carpets have a high reputation. Their most notable characteristic is their durability: the knot density is not especially high as rather thick yarn is used, but the weft threads were beaten with a special iron comb which makes the pile very compact. Bijar carpets must always be rolled up, not folded, as the weft threads may otherwise snap. The Turkish knot is generally used, though the Persian knot also occurs. Patterns are numerous, but the herati motif is especially common, most often on a red ground.

Above: Persian carpet, Bakhtiari, 19th century; private collection. The ground is of natural (undyed) camel hair. *Left:* Bakhtiari carpet of more typical pattern, with the ground divided into differently coloured sections. *Right:* Persian carpet, Bijar, 19th century; private collection. These carpets are generally of exceptional quality.

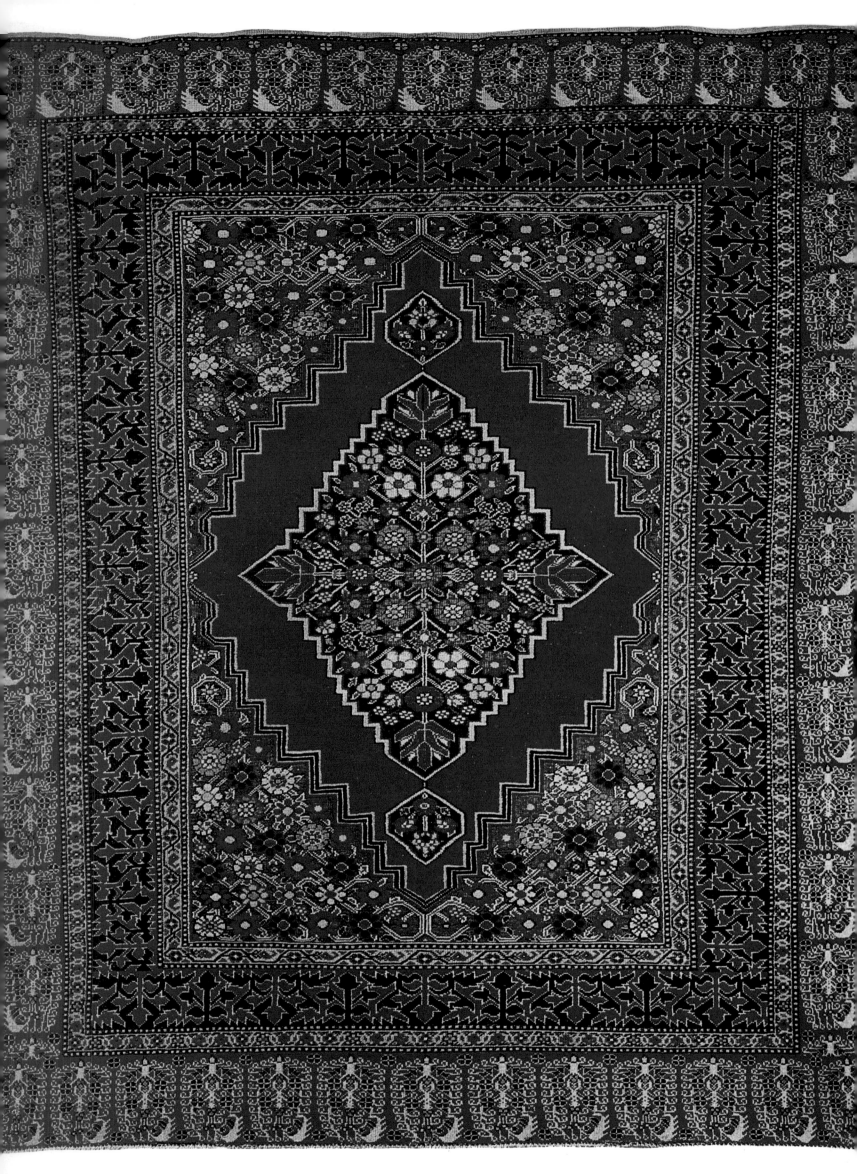

Fereghan. The plateau to the south-west of Teheran contains numerous carpet-making villages. Old Fereghan carpets are eagerly sought by collectors, and were especially popular in 19th-century England. The most common pattern is the herati motif repeated all over a red or dark blue field; in fact, so characteristic is this device that the herati is sometimes called the Fereghan pattern. Another type has a central medallion on a relatively uncluttered field. The borders are especially attractive, featuring a delicate light green occasionally. A 19th-century specimen in a private collection in Milan has —unusually— a rose-red field entirely undecorated except for the corners, with a border consisting of nine closely decorated bands. The Persian knot is traditional, but the Turkish knot occurs occasionally on more recent examples.

Three splendid Feraghan carpets of the 19th century. They come from a large number of villages and display great variety.

Next pages: **Two further specimens from the Feraghan region, with rich red ground, large central medallion, and spacious borders.**

Hamadan. This city of western Persia gives its name to a variety of carpets, individually distinguishable only by experts, from surrounding villages. Antique Hamadan carpets are of high quality. The most typical design is a central medallion on a flower-covered field, and colours tend to be limited. There are many others. Modern Hamadans are of poorer quality; they employ the Turkish knot rather than the traditional Persian knot.

Heriz. Like Hamadan, Heriz includes carpets from many villages, besides the city itself. Among them are Tabriz (see below), Bakshis, Gorevan and Serab. At one time very fine silk carpets were made at Heriz. The wool carpets are often rather coarse, though tough, and the commonest pattern has a large, geometric central medallion, usually on a red field. Modern Heriz carpets are made with the Turkish knot.

Antique Hamadan carpets. The name incorporates a great number of types. Camel hair was widely used in this area.

Isfahan. The old Safavid produced what were perhaps the finest carpets ever made in the 16th and 17th centuries. They are, of course, museum pieces. With the Afghan invasion in the early 18th century, the art was destroyed, and not fully revived until about 1900. However, it soon regained something of its old reputation thanks to beautiful floral designs based on traditional patterns. The Persian knot is used, often with very high density, and some carpets are still made with a silk pile. A famous type known as Joshagan, from a village to the north, is often called 'Isfahan'. It includes 'tree' carpets, with the whole field covered by ferns, leaves and branches.

In the early years of this century the art of carpet-making was revived in Isfahan with considerable success, as the rich examples displayed on these pages demonstrate. Patterns were largely based on the designs of the old Safavid court workshops. *Next pages:* **A) In this garden carpet, probably from Isfahan, happy use is made of blue in the main outlines. B) Persian carpet, Kashan; private collection. The restrained colours and calmly ordered design, executed with timeless patience, give this piece its simple serenity.**

29

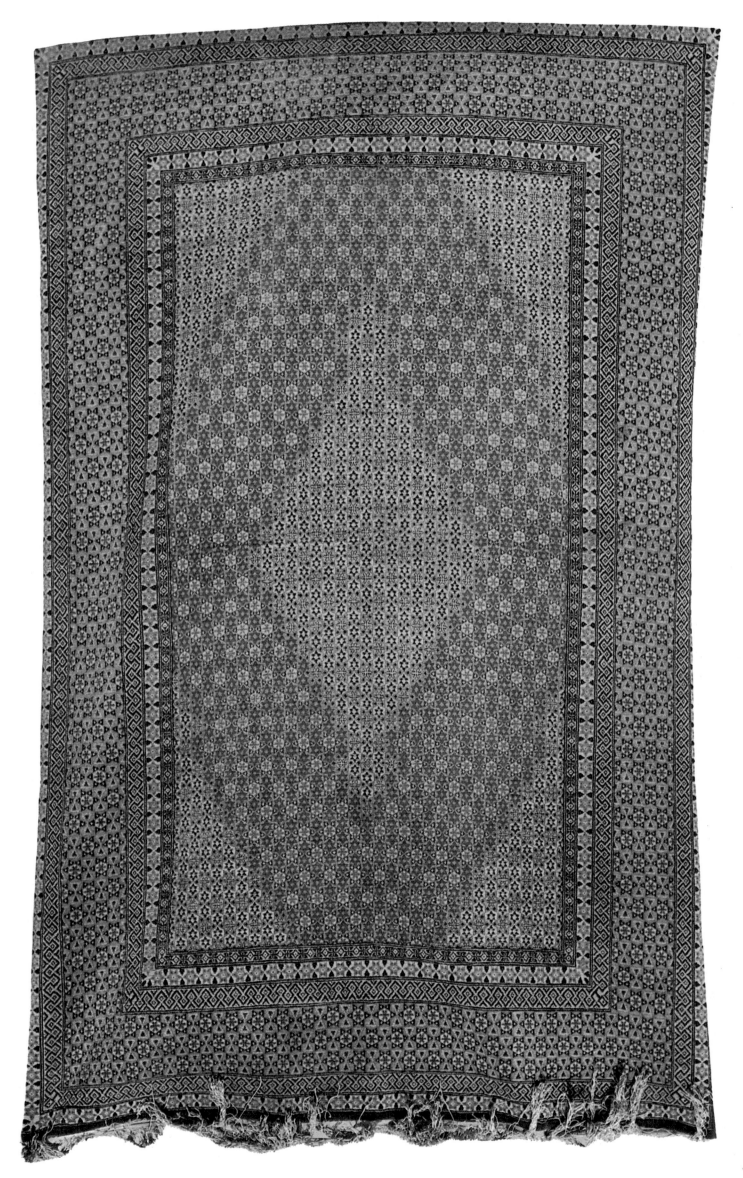

Kashan. Kashan is another great carpet-making centre, where the carpets from the Ardebil mosque were probably made. It is a poor city, whose people lived largely in cellars to escape the heat, but the revival of carpet-making in the late 19th century showed little decline from the great period of the 16th and 17th centuries. Perhaps the finest Persian carpets in recent years have come from Kashan. They include silk prayer rugs and some large and magnificent floral carpets made with Australian merino wool. They have a central medallion; red and blue are the commonest colours. The Persian knot is used and the weft is sometimes of silk.

Four Kashan carpets made in the 20th century, exemplifying the high standards preserved in Kashan despite a period of several centuries during which the craft languished. *Next pages:* **Prayer rug (18th cent.) at the principal mosque of Isfahan.**

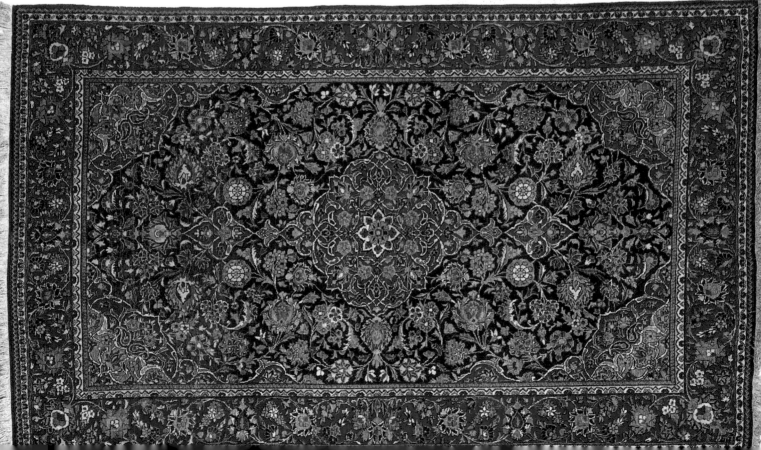

Khorassan. This large region of north-east Persia includes Mesheds, Birjands and Turkbaffs (i.e. 'Turkish knot', uncommon in this area). The herati pattern is frequently adopted and the boteh motif also features prominently in both field and borders. In many villages it appears to have been customary to weave three threads, instead of one, in the cotton weft every few rows.

Three carpets from Khorassan, dating from the late 19th and early 20th centuries. In the lively and accomplished example *above*, from a private collection in Teheran, the use of yellow in the corners of the field helps to make the pattern 'fly' outwards, suggesting flowers unfolding. The plain red ground (*right*) suggests a window in a mosque; the repeated rosettes in the detail *far right*, an endless garden. *Below right:* A modern carpet with the *mina khani* motif.

Kirman. An ancient city situated in the largely desert country of south-east Persia, Kirman includes the products of a number of outlying villages whose craftsmen are famous for their expertise. Although carpet-making is no doubt an ancient tradition, no Kirman carpets are known earlier than mid-19th century. The designs are invariably floral and highly naturalistic, sometimes with a large central medallion, and the colours are usually restrained. Without losing their local distinction, Kirman designers adapted easily to Western taste. The most magnificent specimens, called Kirman-Lavers, come from the village of Rava.

Right: **A magnificent Kirman carpet.** *Above:* **The *herati* motif in a carpet from western Iran.** *Below:* **Bold stripes and geometric pattern in a typical nomadic kilim.**

40

Lilihan. Carpets from this town were woven by people of Armenian origin who settled in the area after the First World War. The floral design in stylized geometric motifs is closer to the Caucasus than to Persia, and the general quality is moderate, though distinguished by fine colours. Manufacture appears to have declined in recent years.

Qum and Nain. Very high-quality carpets have been made in the city of Qum for perhaps the last half-century. The Persian knot is used in uncommonly high density. Patterns range over the whole Persian tradition, though an ivory ground for the field and a predominantly blue border are characteristic of many examples, and both the Shah Abbas pattern and the boteh motif are frequently employed. Occasionally silk is introduced into the pile for highly detailed parts of the design. Although Qum is about 300 km from Nain, their carpets are closely similar and of equally fine quality.

Left and *above:* **Three fine, comparatively modern carpets, in markedly different styles, from the distinguished carpet-making centre of Qum.**
Right: **Nain carpet, 20th century; private collection. This is a good example of recent Iranian carpet production, with much concentrated floral detail in the medallion pattern.**

Saruk. Rugs bearing the name of this town are well known in the United States where they were imported in large numbers in the 1930s. They have attractive floral patterns, often on a light red ground, and are obviously designed for export. Due to chemical treatment, they do not wear very well, and they do not, in fact, come from Saruk itself. However, the rugs of Josan, a smaller centre where high standards have been maintained and the distinctive designs of antique Saruk rugs are still followed, are exceptional. Antique Saruks are very fine and dense and are usually in bold floral designs with central medallion and broad bordering band flanked by narrow guards. The Persian knot is always used and the predominant colours are rich and dark.

Five Saruk carpets. These are made in virtually all the classic Persian shapes and in a variety of patterns, usually floral with a central medallion and often a light-coloured ground. Those made before about 1920, including the carpets shown here, are usually hard-wearing, with the weft threads well beaten down.

Senneh. From the vicinity of this town, which gave its name to the Persian knot (though the Turkish knot has been used in recent times), come some of the most finely woven of all Persian carpets. Traditionally, only wool from young lambs was used and with warp and weft —sometimes silk— very fine, knot density is extremely high. The pile is short and the carpets very supple. An all-over pat-

tern of repeated motifs such as the boteh or herati is the commonest design, though there is sometimes a central medallion. It is curious that these thoroughly typical Persian carpets come from an area which

Senneh is one of the most famous carpet-producing centres, and an antique Senneh in good condition

is virtually priceless. The brilliant colours and imprecise knotting of a modern piece, like that *above*, create a rather striking contrast with the more distinguished products of an earlier period, *left* and *above left*. Senneh carpets generally have an all-over pattern; the central-medallion type is comparatively rare.

is otherwise more closely allied to Turkish or Caucasian traditions.

Shiraz. The capital of the province of Fars and centre of carpet-making in southern Iran, Shiraz includes a number of individual types, such as Afshar, Kashkay and Niris. Good-quality wool is used, often for warp and weft as well as pile, and decoration tends to be simple and stylized, verging on geometric. The most characteristic feature of Shiraz carpets is a diamond in the centre of the field, or a line of such diamonds from top to bottom. Both Persian and Turkish knots are used. The quality is variable, but seldom of the very highest standard. This also applies to the pilgrims' prayer rugs sometimes called Mecca-Shiraz (it was customary for pilgrims to leave them in Mecca).

Sultanabad. This city, now known as Arak, is the centre of a large carpet-making area and includes many towns and villages whose names are applied to individual types. However, names like Arak or Mahal used by dealers indicate the type or quality rather than the place of origin. In modern times the dominant

type throughout the area, especially in Arak itself, has been the Saruk (see above). A somewhat older type known as Sultanabad has floral designs often in the Shah Abbas pattern. Modern Sultanabads and Mahals are often of good quality despite a high degree of industrialization.

Three antique Shiraz carpets. They come from a wide area and are woven on horizontal looms by different nomadic tribes in the province of Fars. The decorative motifs tend to be simple and geometric and the quality is variable, with knot density usually on the low side. Red is the commonest ground colour.
Next pages: **A fine Tabriz carpet dating from the late 18th or early 19th century; private collection. Tabriz carpets are generally the work of urban craftsmen, and the best examples are among the most elegant of all Persian carpets.**

46

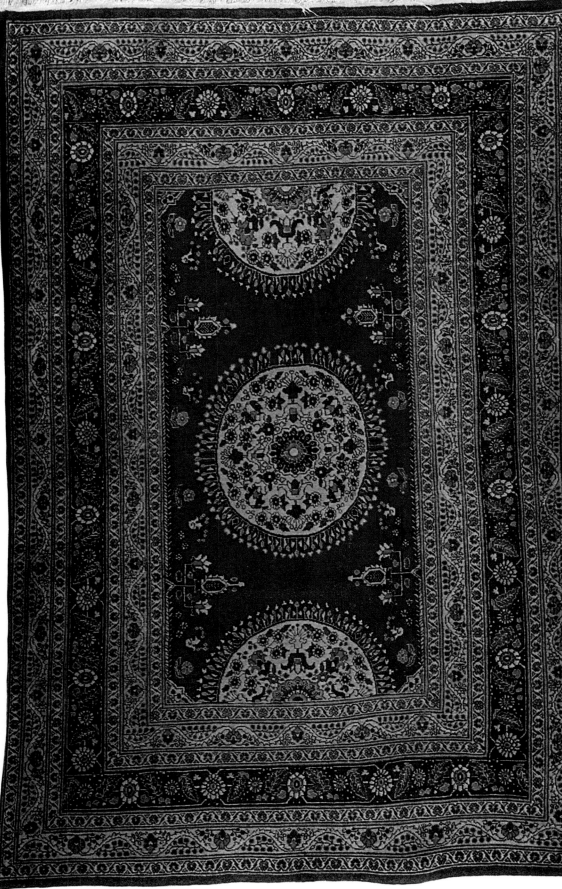

Tabriz. This is the second largest city in Iran and an important centre for the making and selling of a wide range of carpets. Antique Tabriz carpets, which are broadly similar in design to those of Kashan or Kirman, are eagerly sought. They were usually made with the Persian knot, though the Turkish knot has long since taken over —except in some excellent reproductions of old silk hunting carpets. Carpet-making developed here largely in response to export demands in the mid-19th century, and is now organized along industrial lines.

Left: Persian carpet, Tabriz, early 20th century; private collection. The central medallion is carried outwards, like ripples from a stone thrown into a pool, and is echoed in the four corners. *Above*: **Persian carpet, Tabriz, early 19th century; Golestan Museum, Teheran.**

The circular medallion is a characteristic Tabriz device and here, repeated in semicircles at either end, suggests the rising and setting of the sun.

Teheran. The modern capital of Iran has no long tradition of carpet-making. However, some of the finest modern oriental carpets, similar to those of Isfahan, are made here. No doubt the finest of all are to be seen only in private houses in Iran.

Left: **Teheran has become a centre for fine carpets in recent times.**

Above: **Bukhara carpet, Yomud, late 19th century.** *Below:* **Persian carpet, Veramin (near Teheran), about 1900. It is decorated with the *mina khani* motif.**

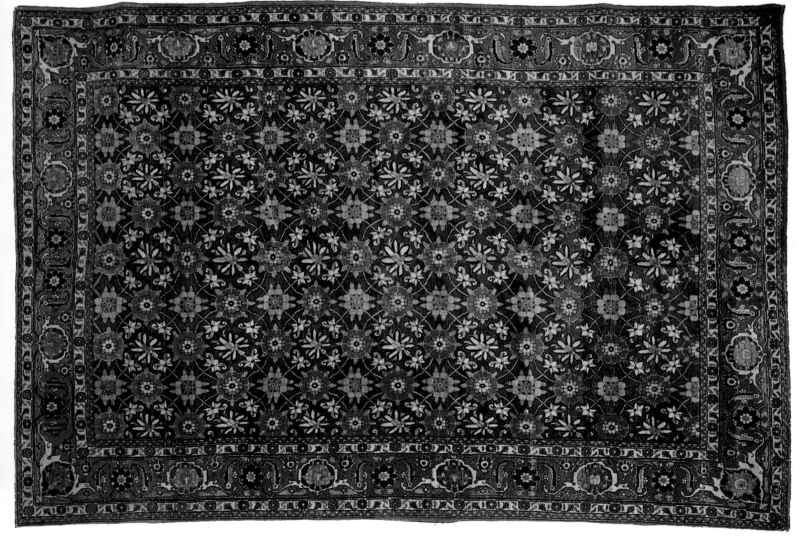

TURKEY

Carpet-making in Turkey was perhaps never so prolific a craft as it was in Persia, and the decline in modern times has been, on the whole, more severe. The great age of carpet-making coincided with the great age of the Ottoman empire, from the 15th to the 17th centuries. A decline in quality in the 18th century was partially checked in the 19th, under the stimulus of Western demand, but most recent Turkish carpets —since the third quarter of the 19th century— are quite different from the antique pieces. There is one technical characteristic which conveniently marks this division. Before about 1870 cotton was not generally available and the warp and weft were therefore of wool or goat hair. No Turkish carpet with cotton warp and weft can be much older than 100 years.

In the modern period too, the strict limits regarding pattern were abandoned. Antique Turkish carpets, with a few exeptions, have geometric patterns based on floral motifs. The colour green is seldom found except in prayer rugs, and most carpets, not only prayer rugs, are comparatively small.

The popularity of Turkish carpets in Renaissance Europe has already been mentioned, and it is largely through the work of painters that we can most easily admire the works of the old Anatolian craftsmen. Venice, as the chief entrepôt for Eastern trade, was particularly richly provided. When Cardinal Wolsey was furnishing his palace at Hampton Court in the 1520s he ordered sixty Turkish carpets from a Venetian merchant.

As in Persia, the nomenclature of Turkish carpets, based on supposed places of origin, is complex. There are between thirty and forty different types, but many can only be identified by experts and, in general, there is less variation than in Persia. All use the Turkish or Ghiordes knot.

Bergama. A red thread is often used in the weft and it is usually visible on the back. Colours are strong, size small, shape sometimes square; many have a geometric central medallion. Bergama is the ancient Pergamum, and some carpets appeared on the market in the early 20th century called Pergamos. Rather slack and undistinguished, they were probably made elsewhere.

Ghiordes. From this town, the ancient Gordium where Alexander cut the Gordian knot that no one could untie, come the finest Turkish carpets. The prayer rugs are most famous. They have a distinctive and harmonious design, characteristic borders of many narrow bands decorated with small flowers. A lamp often appears in the mihrab. The antique secular rugs are less distinguished: one unusual feature is the comparatively common use of green. Modern Ghiordes carpets bear no relation to the traditional types.

Above: **Detail of an Anatolian carpet of the 16th century.** *Above right:* **Turkish carpet, Bergama, 18th century; Jerusalem Museum. The bold colours, square shape and simple geometric forms suggest its nomadic origin.** *Below:* **Prayer rugs are associated particularly with Anatolia.**

Hereke. The sultan's workshops in this city not far from Constantinople produced immensely valuable silk rugs which are entirely in the Persian tradition, though using the Turkish knot; the weavers originally came from Kirman.

Kirshehir. Prayer rugs from this and adjacent places on the central Anatolian plain are noted for their magnificent colours; the borders are generally wide and the overall formality or their appearance is sometimes challenged by idiosyncratic, assymetrical touches.

Above: Turkish carpet, detail, the 'Saltings' carpet, Hereke, late 19th century; Victoria and Albert Museum, London. An example of the work, quite divorced from Turkish traditions, produced at the court workshops in Hereke in the latter years of the Ottoman Empire. The prayer rug (*far left*) and the floral carpet (detail *left*) are also from Hereke.
Right: Anatolian prayer rug, late 19th century. Such pieces have no affinity with Turkish traditions; the vase-of-flowers motif is of Persian derivation.

58

Kula. Prayer rugs similar to those of Ghiordes (only 80 km distant), which means of the highest quality, were made here. Some can be distinguished by a design in which the mihrab is set not at the top of the field but about two-thirds up. 'Cemetery' or 'tomb' rugs from Kula have a pattern of cypress trees and small buildings.

Ladik. The rare and beautiful prayer rugs (there seem to be few modern examples) of Ladik (ancient Laodicea) can often be recognized by the pattern of the mihrab, which is often three-arched, sometimes stepped, and has a rectangular panel above and, often, one below containing stylized tulips.

Kayseri carpets occur in both large and small sizes and in a variety of patterns. Some are woven entirely of silk. The three examples here demonstrate the variety, and also the lack of originality, in Kayseri designs. The carpet at *right*, for instance, is essentially Persian in character, and suggests Tabriz rather than central Anatolia. *Next pages:* a) Anatolian prayer rug, probably Ladik (the inverted tulips at the base are a famous Ladik 'trademark'). b) A loosely woven Anatolian floral carpet.

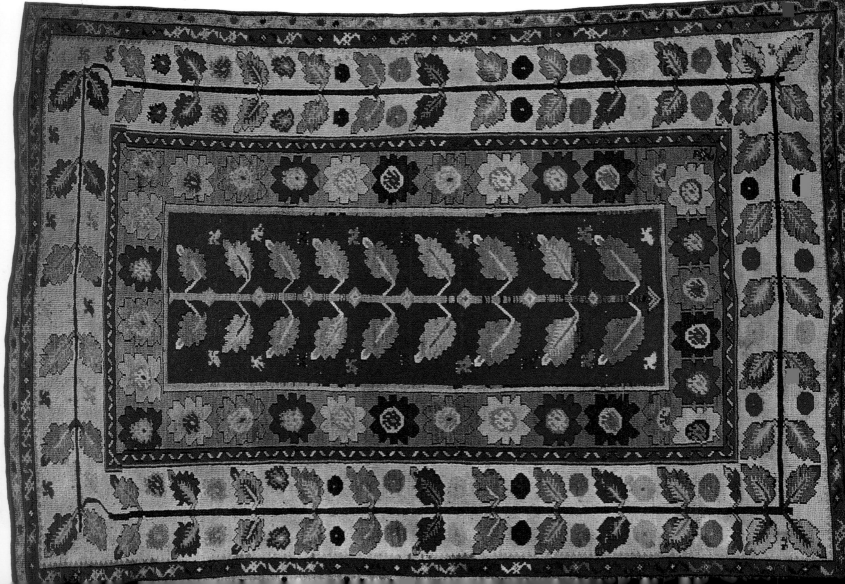

Melas. This is a marketing centre for many villages which formerly produced highly stylized prayer rugs in which the mihrab, frequently on a brownish-red field, is diamond-shaped, with decorative motifs in white or cream.

Sivas. Characteristic products of this central Anatolian city vary considerably. Unexpectedly, the commonest types are in the Persian tradition. Antique examples are notable for their fine workmanship, and pale colours are often adopted.

Opposite: **A pair of old Melas rugs.** *Below:* **Sivas carpet in the Persian style.**

Yuruk. Made by Kurds in eastern Turkey, they share characteristics with carpets from adjacent regions in Iran and the Caucasus. Motifs are strictly geometrical, with much use of Greek-key designs; frequently, the field bears three diamond-shaped medallions.

There are various less specific names often used by dealers or in books. 'Anatolian' is applied to practically any Turkish carpet of uncertain origin, more particularly to carpets from centres south-east of Ankara. 'Smyrna' usually means poorish, modern carpets, mainly from western Turkey; Smyrna (Izmir) is the place of export. 'Transylvania' carpets are allegedly those left in that region by the Ottoman army in the 17th century. 'Syrian' or 'Damascan' are fine antique Turkish carpets that passed through Syria on their way to the West.

Left: Detail of one of the most beautiful Ushak carpets of the 17th century. **Above:** Another Ushak carpet, 16th century.
Right: Anatolian prayer rug. Modernization has led to a decline in carpet-making in Turkey in this century in spite of some government encouragement (less effective than in Iran). Many of the traditional features of Turkish carpets have been abandoned. For instance, 20th-century production includes comparatively large carpets, which are rare in the earlier period. Religious structures, concerning the colour green or the depiction of living creatures, are no longer significant.

CAUCASUS

This is the area of the Soviet Union between the Black Sea and the Caspian Sea, where life is, for the most part, still fairly simple and close to the soil (or, indeed, to the rock, for the terrain is inhospitable). The region is inhabited by a variety of peoples, Christian and Muslim. Until the early 19th century it was part of Persia, while there has also been much interchange of population with Anatolia (Turkey). For these reasons, Caucasian carpets are not always easily identified by their design, and they often cause confusion even among experts.

In spite of the great variety of Caucasian carpets, most have a certain resemblance in their rugged, uncompromissing geometry.

From the north-east come the *Chi-Chi* carpets made by the Tchechen. Modern examples are seldom found and they are exclusively collector's pieces, admired equally for their fine workmanship and intricate, mosaic-like design. The borders are distinctive: much use is made of slanting bars and, in the narrower bands, of closely repeated eight-pointed 'stars'.

Daghestan rugs are similarly old and rare. The field is generally divided into diagonal bands, often filled with squares that have a trailing hook at opposite corners. The eight-pointed star may appear in the borders. Daghestan prayer rugs have a distinctive hexagonal niche to the mihrab and, usually, an overall diamond pattern.

Traditional Caucasian rugs have a stark and jagged geometricity which many collectors find especially attractive. Although there are comparatively few long-established types, classification is often difficult owing to the nomadic way of life of the people and the profusion of modern dealers' names. *Here:* details of a fine Chi-Chi. *Right:* Two Daghestan rugs incorporating the *boteh* motifs. *Next pages:* This piece typefies the bold colours, simple forms and fine weaving of the Caucasus.

Derbent rugs are valuable because they are rare. Otherwise, they are not outstanding: colours are rich and the quality rather coarse.

In the southermost area of *Karabagh* the design, as one would expect, is Persian-influenced, with occasionally a strong suggestion of Savonnerie.

Above: **A beautiful Karabagh carpet, essentially Persian in character.** *Below:* **Caucasian carpet, probably Kuba (southern Daghestan).** *Left:* **In some carpets from the southern Caucasus, figures of animals and birds —somewhat stylized in this example— do occur.**

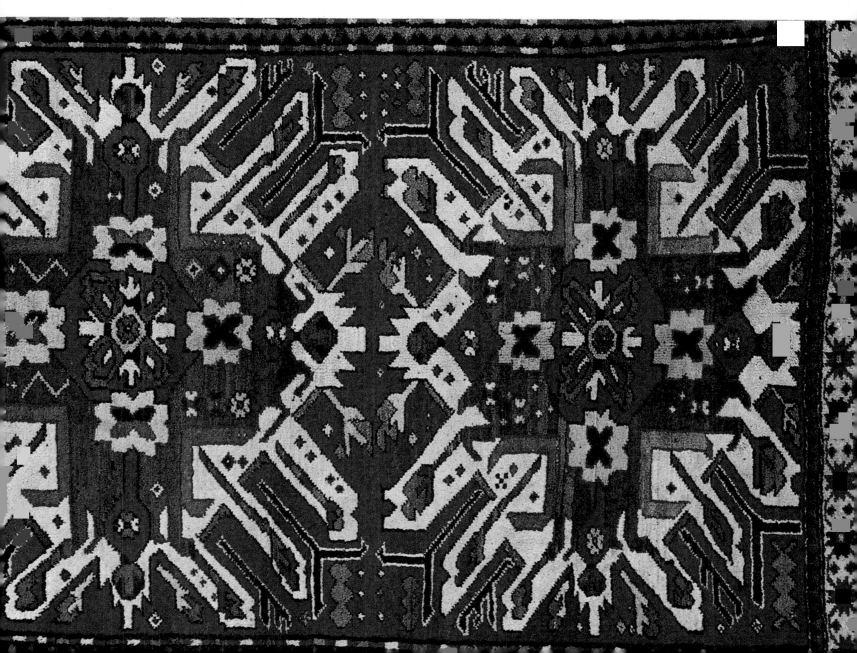

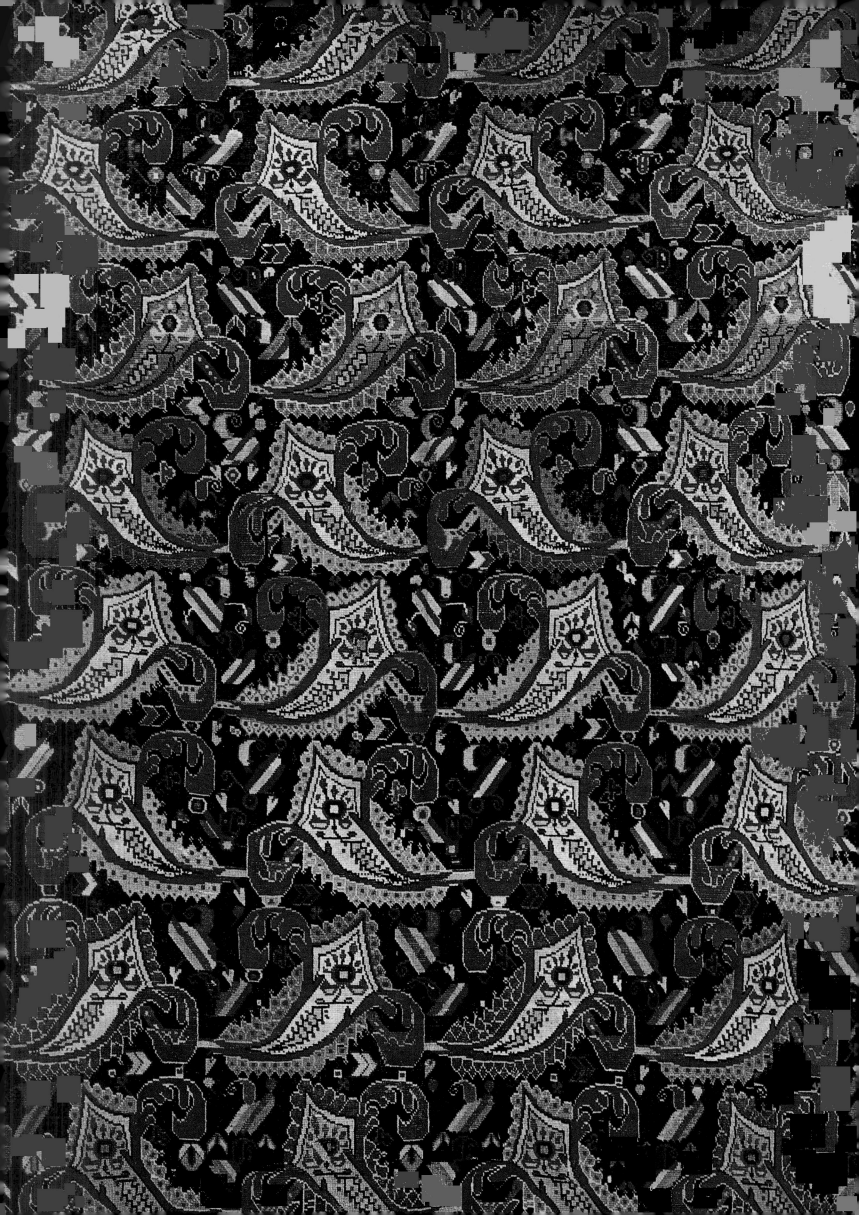

Left: Caucasian carpet, Karabagh, 19th century. Karabagh lies on the Iranian border, which explains the largely Persian inspiration of the carpets, but they are chiefly notable for distinctive colour, in particular a vivid shade of magenta. Too rich for European tastes, old Karabagh carpets were sometimes deliberately darkened for Western consumers.

Above and *below:* Two Karabagh carpets, showing a mixture of Persian and Chinese influence.

Right: A Karabagh carpet that could almost be French, clearly designed for a Western market.

Probably the most famous names among Caucasian carpets are *Kazak* and *Shirvan*. Traditionally, Kazaks are highly coloured (like many Caucasian carpets) with free use of white. The field often contains one or three geometric medallions of unusual shape and the decoration is always very formal. Among their other virtues, they are very hard-wearing, despite a rather shaggy pile.

Like Kazaks, Shirvan carpets are difficult to identify for sure because they employ motifs common in other parts of the region. Output was large, and dealers tend to apply the name Shirvan to almost any Caucasian carpet of problematic origin.

There is probably more scope for

Above and *left*: Samarkand carpets, Khotan, 19th century. Most Samarkand carpets have a Chinese appearance, with large medallions, as in this piece. The example below, however, though betraying Chinese taste in the central border band, is more closely linked with the floral carpets of Iran. *Above right*: Caucasian rug, Kazak, 19th century. The slightly eccentric medallions are often found on these tough little carpets. *Below right*: Caucasian carpet, Seichur, 19th century; private collection. The transverse cross is characteristic of Seichur, as is the latch-key or 'running-dog' device on a white or ivory ground in the border. Such pieces are extremely rare, though the type was made at a later date in other parts of the Caucasus.

confusion among Caucasian carpets than any others. On the whole, the traditional varieties persisted until about 1920, but modern carpets bearing the traditional names often have little or no connection with the antiques. For example, in recent years many carpets described as 'Kazak' have been exported from the Soviet Union, but none of them compares with the originals in quality and many adopt designs which are unknown among traditional Kazaks.

A number of other names often occur in books or dealers' catalogues in connection with Caucasian carpets. The term 'Armenian' for example, ought to apply, perhaps, to a group of ancient carpets made in the south with patterns based on highly stylized animals, which are no longer to be found commercially. In fact the term is often used as a synonym for Caucasian.

There is one other type of Caucasian rug which must be mentioned, known as *Sumak*. The name comes from Shemakha, a town in the south-east, but Sumaks are made all over the region (and are made nowadays in many other places too). Sumaks are not knotted; they are weft-faced carpets, like killims, with the decoration made by weft threads turned around the warp in a manner akin to embroidery. As these threads continue only as far as a colour change, they are comparatively short: long ends are left on the back so that, viewed from the reverse side, a Sumak rug looks like a dog's dinner. The technique is at least 2,000 years old; the famous 'Springtime of Chosroes' carpet (6th century AD) was a carpet or this type.

Traditional Sumaks are extremely attractive —some would say the most beautiful of all Caucasian carpets. All the characteristic Caucasian motifs occur, and patterns are strongly geometric.

Sumak rugs are woven all over the Caucasus. Like kilims, they consist only or warp and weft: there is no knotted pile. There are normally two threads to the weft, one forming the decoration and the other serving to strengthen the fabric, as in knotted carpets. The 19th-century Sumak, *left*, is a typical example, with geometric medallions and running-dog border motif.

OTHER REGIONS

Turkestan, the name of a historic region comprising, roughly, the area of the Soviet Union east of the Caspian Sea and bordering on Afghanistan, is a name seldom heard now except in reference to oriental carpets. Turkoman carpets, including those from Turkestan and Afghanistan, generally use the Persian knot, and the most characteristic design is of rows of guls or octagons in various forms on a brownish-red field.

The great name in Turkoman carpets is of course *Bukhara,* a name which, like 'Persian', was at one time virtually a synonym for oriental carpets in general. Bukhara, the great Muslim cultural centre of Central Asia, was the chief market for carpets woven over a very wide area, and there are half-a-dozen generally recognized types. They include the so-called Royal Bukharas —a name invented by Western dealers to signify fine quality— which are made by the nomadic Tekke and are perhaps the most finely woven of all oriental carpets. Tekke Bukhara prayer rugs, sometimes known as Princess Bukharas, are no less fine, and their distinctive design —with the motif usually described as a candlestick, in deepest blue, occupying a quartered field — is easily recognised. Equally valuable, and more rare, are Pinde Bukharas, especially the prayer rugs (known as *hatchly*).

In recent years, the main source of Bukhara carpets has been *Pakistan.* Known as Moris, they are made in various parts of that country and have enjoyed government aid as a valuable export industry. A fine, lustrous, Cashmere (Kashmir) wool is employed —at one time mostly imported as yarn from Britain— and the knot density is very high, sometimes as much as 500 knots per square inch. Government subsidy plus low manufacturing costs explain their comparatively low price and this, combined with their indisputable quality — makes them a very attractive proposition. Nevertheless, they are of course merely commercial reproductions, with no real tradition behind them, and in a way difficult to define (though easy enough to observe given the opportunity of direct comparison) they lack the warmth and harmony of old Bukharas.

To many people, in Britain especially, perhaps, a Bukhara is *the* oriental carpet. You can't go into many English homes without seeing one (or a least a fair imitation). The Tekke Bukhara, like those *below* and *above right*, is one of the most notable categories. *Below right:* Hatchlie, or Turkoman prayer rug, 19th century.

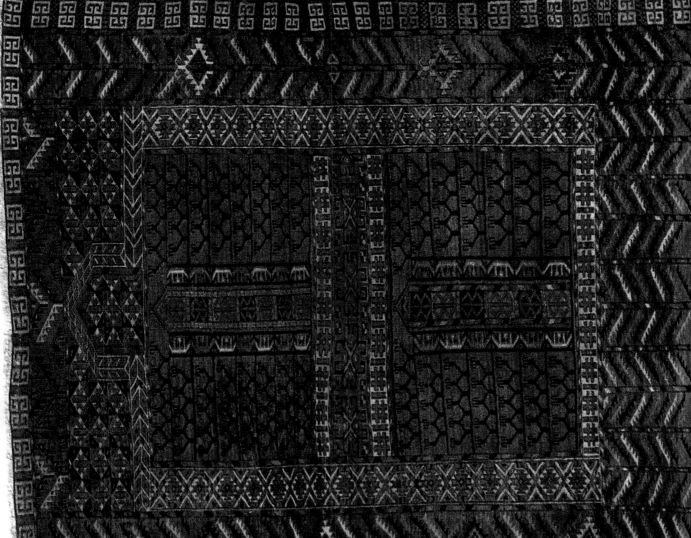

Three Caucasian carpets. The example opposite, with its double *boteh* pattern, belongs to the first half of the 19th century; the examples on this page are more modern.

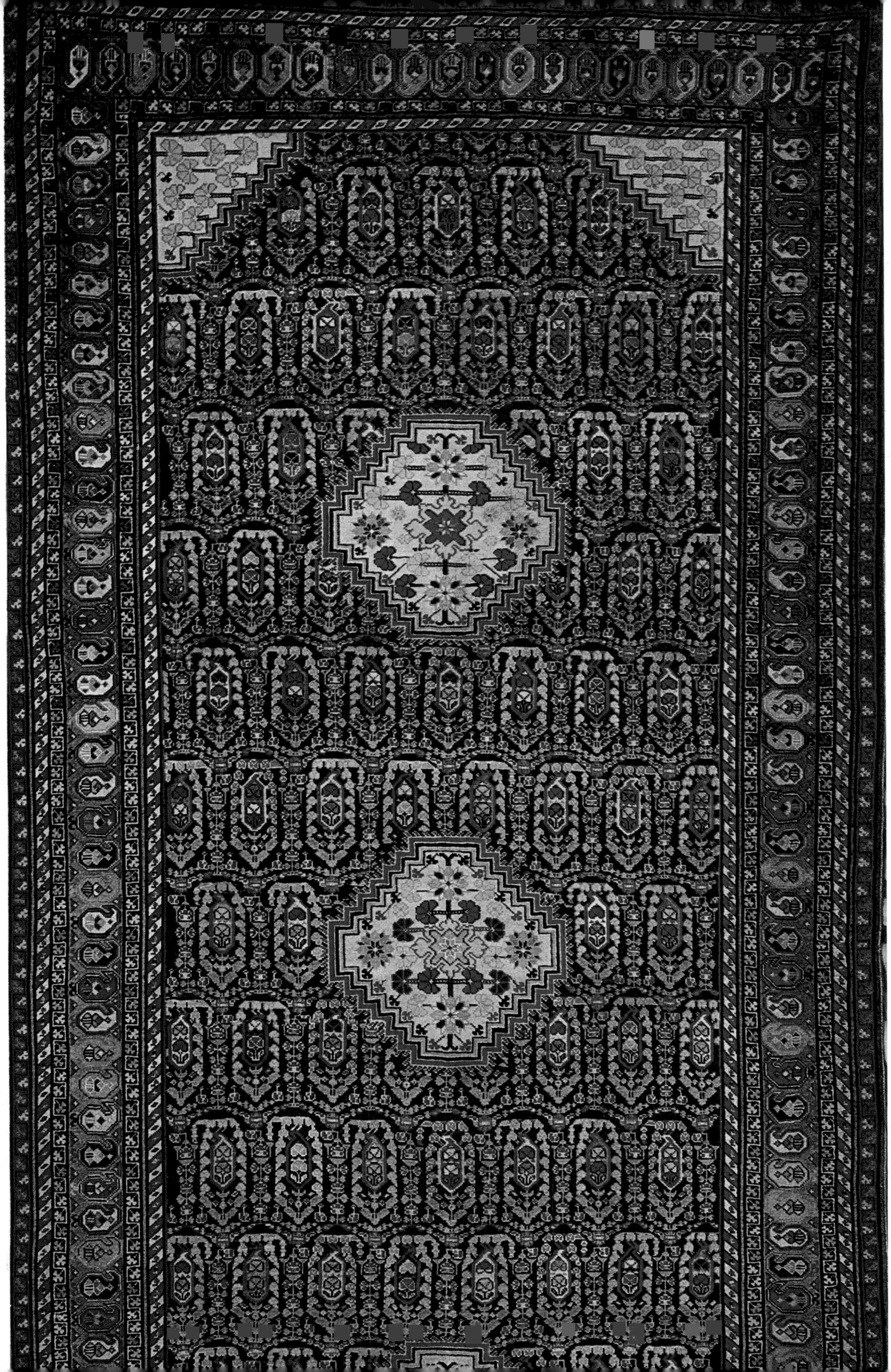

Pakistan also produces copies of Persian carpets, particularly those of Tabriz and Kirman, which are likewise of high quality. The one important traditional type of carpet emanating from what is now Pakistan is that of *Baluchistan*. The original weavers were nomads also found in Turkestan and Afghanistan; they are similar to other Turkoman carpets though generally more sombre in appearance: the usual Turkoman red is less evident, and is often replaced by a dark blue.

Afghan carpets have also acquired considerable popularity in the West. Though no longer made by nomads, they are basically similar to other Turkoman carpets. They include a type sometimes called Beshir Bukhara, made on both sides of the border between Pakistan and the Soviet Union, and Khiva Bukhara, nowadays made only in Afghanistan and Pakistan. Some of these are comparatively large pieces, and are probably the most popular. The design is an orderly series of the gul motif, quartered and woven in two colours, on a deep red field.

Yomud Bukharas were traditionally made over a wide area, though the main source today is Pakistan. They include a particularly distinctive lattice-like design which is suggestive of Caucasian patterns. More common examples have small white guls on a quartered field of deep red. The candlestick motif is also employed, notably on prayer rugs.

The Yomud people range over most of central Asia, and old Yomud carpets of good quality are still relatively common. The Yomud weavers preferred a rich, deepish red for the field, generally with small medallions or guls.

Both the Turkish and the Persian knots were used; indeed, it has been alleged that examples exist in which both knots can be found in the same carpet!

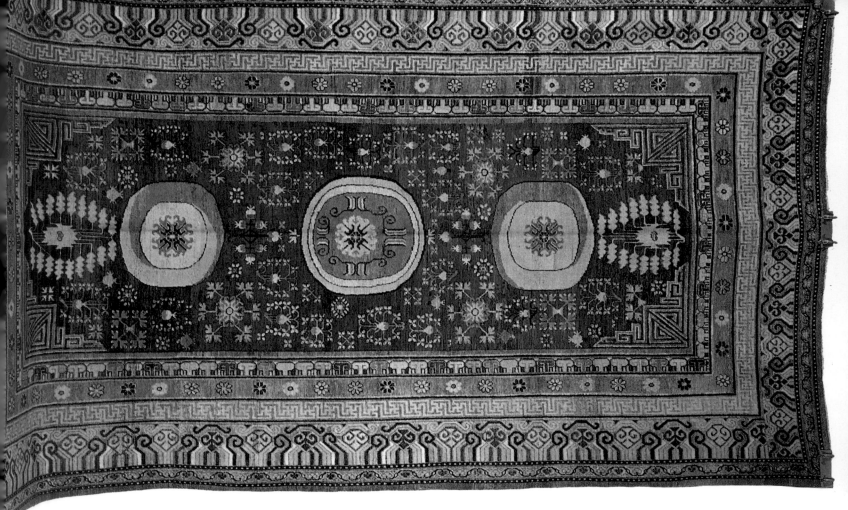

One other centre of Turkoman carpets should be mentioned, Samarkand. This is the market for carpets in the eastern part of the region, which are essentially Chinese in type, like the carpets of Nepal and Tibet.

Today, carpets are also made in very large numbers in *India* (including *Kashmir*). Indeed, India may well be the largest single producer, after Iran.

The history of carpet-making in India is curiously episodic. Briefly, the modern industry dates from the mid-19th century, when factories were set up by Bristish and, later, U.S. enterprises. Large numbers of carpets, on the whole of good

quality, have been produced continuously ever since, under a bewildering variety of names. The United States has been the main export market, and a large proportion of the carpets produced are not oriental in any meaningful sense, being copies of 18th-century French designs. So-called 'Indian Aubussons', not knotted but worked with a needle, come mainly from Kashmir. Copies of traditional Chinese carpets are also made.

There are certain especially notable carpets from the modern period, in particular *Agra* carpets, very large, finely knotted pieces of Persian-influenced design though employing some very 'un-

Persian' colours; they were made at Agra in the late 19th century.

Between about 1650 and 1850 Indian carpets were of no very great interest, but in the century earlier some of the most magnificent of all oriental carpets were made at the workshops established in various cities by the early Mughal emperors (notably Akbar the Great, a contemporary of Shah Abbas). The most magnificent floral carpets, similar to those Isfahan, employing the Persian knot (and possibly made by craftsmen from the Safavid capital), were produced at *Lahore* (now in Pakistan). There is one splendid example in Girdlers' Hall in London. Such pieces do not appear on the market and can be seen only in museums. There is, for example, a gorgeous floral prayer rug which (despite the obvious Persian influence) could only have been made in Mughal India, in the Österreichisches Museum, Vienna.

We know that weaving was established in ancient *Egypt* nearly 5,000 years ago, and Herodotus described professional carpet-making there, but the great period of carpet-making in Egypt (and to some extent in Morocco) coincided with Ottoman Turkish rule, in the 16th and 17th centuries. Very fine car-

Above: **Samarkand carpet, mid-19th century.** *Left:* **Samarkand carpet, late 19th century, incorporating silver thread.** *Above right:* **Indian floral carpet.** *Right:* **Egyptian prayer rug.**
Last page: **Persian floral prayer rug, Kashkay (Shiraz), late 19th century.**

pets, with silk warp and weft and sometimes silk pile, were then made in Cairo. Many imitated Persian designs; others followed the designs of Damascene metalwork. The name 'Damascene', as noted earlier, was often used in the West to describe oriental carpets of Turkish origin; some of these carpets were made in Syria.

The sultan's workshop in Constantinople is said to have been founded by Egyptian craftsmen in the 16th century: there is a fine example of their work in the splendid collection of the Österreichsisches Museum, which measures nearly 6×3 mètres and employs a great variety of colours in a generally geometric design.

In more recent times Cairo was a major market for oriental carpets which, however, mostly came from Asia Minor.

Carpet-making is an old tradition in other parts of Asia, notably China, and in very recent times it has been adopted as an export industry in countries which have no such tradition. Japan, for example, exports carpets in the French style to the United States in some numbers. Antique oriental carpets of real merit are, inevitably, becoming hard to find. Still, they are sometimes found in unlikely places. A young German lecturer, a collector in a modest way, was wandering in a wood in New York State a few years ago when he came across an old rug dumped with other household refuse. It was somewhat worn and had clearly been discarded because someone had splashed paint on it. Careful cleaning brought most of this off, and the rug was revealed as a fine old Mir piece with an unusually decorative border.

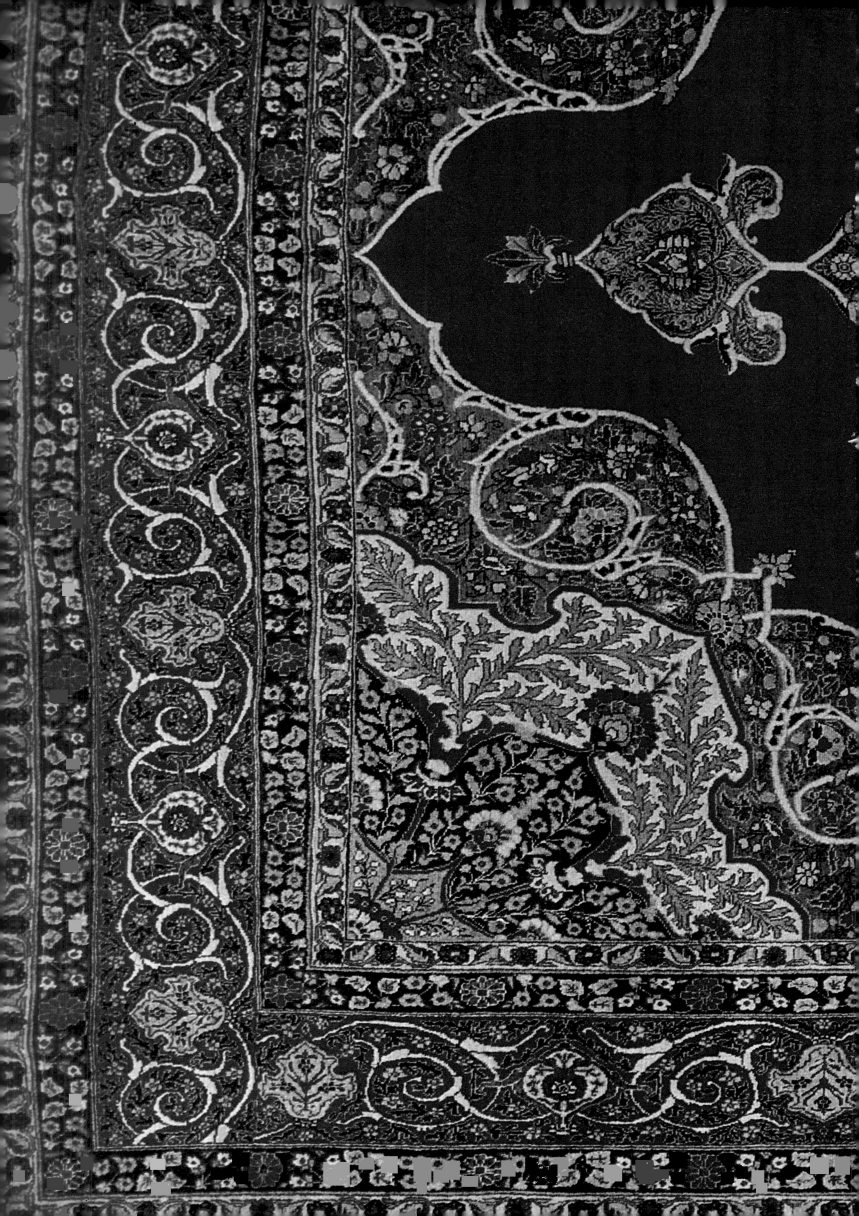